# ANIMALS in DANGER

# Black Rhino

Rod Theodorou

Heinemann Library
Chicago, Illinois

Customer Service  888-454-2279

Visit our website at www.heinemannlibrary.com

Designed by Ron Kamen
Illustrations by Dewi Morris/Robert Sydenham
Originated by Ambassador Litho
Printed in Hong Kong

05 04 03
10 9 8 7 6 5 4 3 2

**Library of Congress Cataloging-in-Publication Data**
Theodorou, Rod.
        Black rhino / Rod Theodorou.
                p.c m. – (Animals in danger)
        Includes bibliographical references (p. )
        ISBN 1-57572-262-3 (lib. bdg.)        ISBN 1-58810-442-7 (pbk. bdg.)
                1. Black rhinoceros—Juvenile literature.  2. Endangered species—Juvenile literature.  [1.
Black rhinoceros.  2. Rhinoceros.  3. Endangered species.]  I. Title.

QL737.U63 T44  2000
599.66'8—dc21
                                                                                                00-026775

**Acknowledgments**
The author and publishers are grateful to the following for permission to reproduce copyright
material:Ardea London, p. 13, Ardea London/ R.F. Porter, p. 23; Corbis, p. 11; FLPA/ Gerard Lacz, p. 4,
FLPA/ David Hosking, pp. 5, 22, FLPA/ W. Wisniewski, p. 6, FLPA/ Eichhorn Zingel, p. 8, FLPA/ Frants
Hartmann, pp. 19, 21; Mike Johnson, p. 4; NHPA/ Martin Harvey,  p. 18, NHPA/ Daryl Balfour, p. 25;
Oxford Scientific Films, p. 16, Oxford Scientific Films/ Daniel J. Cox p. 4, Oxford Scientific Films/ Tom
Leach pp. 7, 9, Oxford Scientific Films/ Stan Osolonski, p. 12, Oxford Scientific Films/ Konrad Wothe,
p. 14, Oxford Scientific Films/ Steve Turner, pp. 15, 24, Oxford Scientific Films/ David Cayless, p. 20;
Still Pictures/ M. & C. Denis-Huot, p.17, Still Pictures/ Michel Gunther, p. 26, Still Pictures/ Roland
Seitre, p. 27

Cover photograph reproduced with permission of Bruce Coleman.
Special thanks to Henning Dräger for his comments in the preparation of this book.

Every effort has been made to contact copyright holders of any material reproduced in this book. Any
omissions will be rectified in subsequent printings if notice is given to the publisher.

# Some words are shown in bold, **like this.** You can find out what they mean by looking in the glossary.

# Contents

# Animals in Danger

blue whale

Bengal tiger

manatee

All over the world, more than 10,000 animal **species** are in danger. Some are in danger because their homes are being destroyed. Many are in danger because people hunt them.

This book is about black rhinos and why they are **endangered**. Unless people learn to **protect** them, black rhinos will become **extinct**. We will only be able to find out about them from books like this.

# What IS a Rhino?

Rhinos are huge **mammals**. There are five different **species** of rhino. The two largest species are the black rhino and the white rhino. This picture shows a white rhino.

They are called black and white rhinos, but both species are gray. White rhinos have wide, square lips. Black rhinos have a pointed, hooked lip like a parrot's beak. This picture shows a black rhino.

# What Does a Rhino Look Like?

Rhinos have huge bodies. They have four short thick legs with three stumpy toes on each leg. Their skin is gray and very thick, like armor. They are heavy, but they can move very quickly.

Some rhinos have only one horn, but the black rhino has two horns. The horns are very hard and are used to protect the rhino from **predators**. A black rhino's horn can grow longer than a baseball bat!

# Where Do Rhinos Live?

AFRICA

Equator

black rhinos
white rhinos

Black and white rhinos both live in Africa. White rhinos like open **savannah** where they can eat lots of grass. Black rhinos like to live on the edge of forests near bushes and trees.

The Indian, Javan, and Sumatran rhinos live in Asia. The Javan and Sumatran rhinos live deep inside rain forests where they can find leaves and fruit to eat. The Indian rhino likes wallowing in cool, muddy swamps and marshes.

# What Do Black Rhinos Eat?

Rhinos are **herbivores**. They only eat plants and fruits. Black rhinos use their hooked lips to pluck off leaves or pull down small trees to eat the fruit.

Black rhinos eat in the morning and late into the evening. They do not like the hot sun. They find a shady place to rest in during the heat of the day.

# Black Rhino Babies

Black rhinos do not live in family groups. They like to live alone and are only together to **mate**. When they have mated the **male** leaves. He does not help take care of the baby.

The **female** usually only has one baby. The baby is called a calf. The calf can stand up about an hour after it is born. It feeds on its mother's milk.

# Caring for the Calf

The calf's horn is only a small bump at first, but it grows quickly. The calf will live with its mother for two or three years, and then it will live on its own.

Hyenas and lions sometimes attack black rhino calves. The mother will charge at any **predator** that comes near her calf. Black rhinos are very fierce when they feel they are in danger.

# Unusual Rhino Facts

Black rhinos cannot see very well, but they have a very good sense of smell. They only have hair on the ends of their tails, on their eyelashes, and on the tips of their ears.

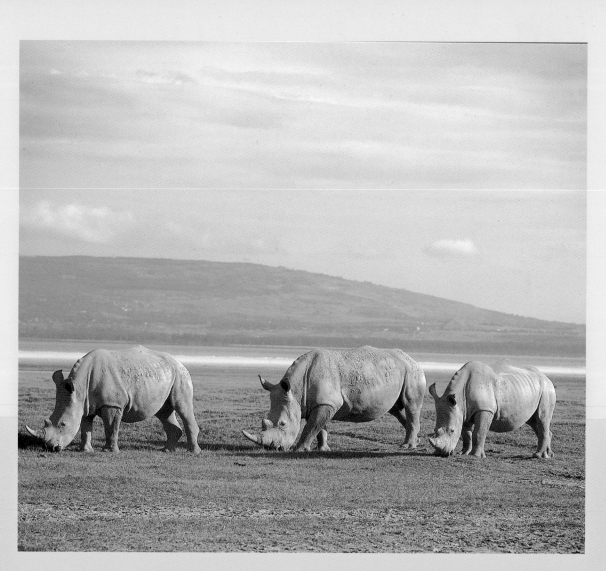

White rhinos live in **herds** and are not very dangerous. Black rhinos live alone and sometimes may charge people who come too close.

# How Many Black Rhinos Are There?

One hundred years ago there were about one million black rhinos in Africa. Now there are fewer than 1,900 of them in the wild, even though they are **protected** by **law**.

Black rhinos are being killed faster than any other large animal on Earth. Over 73,000 have been killed in the last 30 years!

# Why IS the Black Rhino in Danger?

People shoot black rhinos and then cut off their horns to sell them. Many horns go to China to be **ground** down and sold as medicine.

Many horns are sold to a country called Yemen. They are made into the handles of **daggers,** like the ones in this picture.

# How Is the Black Rhino Being Helped?

Many leaders in China and Yemen are trying to stop sales of rhino horn. All African and Asian countries have made rhino hunting against the **law.** This black rhino has his own guard!

**Conservation** groups like the World Wildlife Fund (WWF) and the International Rhino Foundation (IRF) are also working to stop **poaching** and save the rhino.

In some countries black rhinos are caught and their horns are cut off and burned. This does not hurt the rhino, and it stops hunters from **poaching** them until the horns grow back.

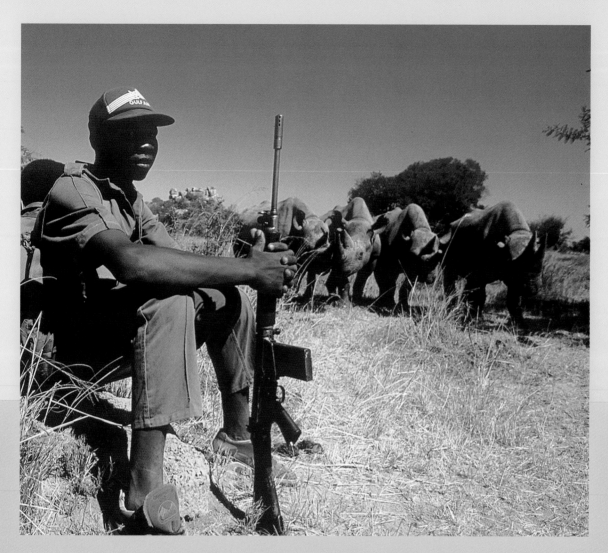

Many African countries have places where the rhinos are **protected** by fences and guards. This is the best way to save the black rhino.

# Rhino Fact File

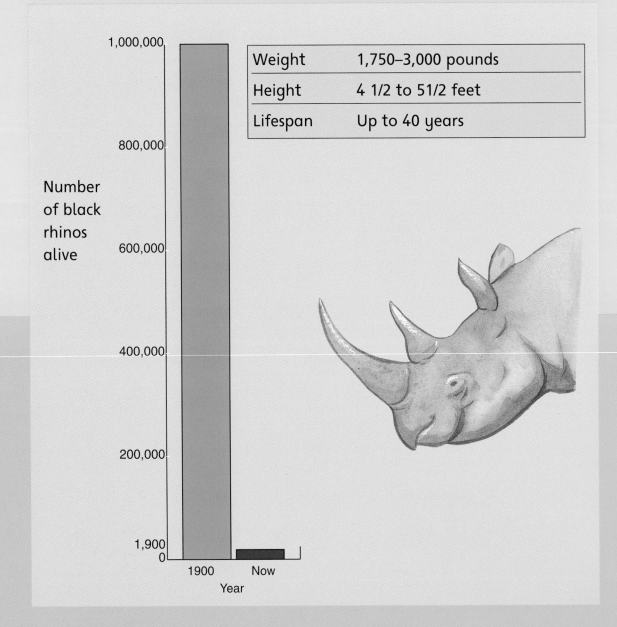

| | |
|---|---|
| Weight | 1,750–3,000 pounds |
| Height | 4 1/2 to 51/2 feet |
| Lifespan | Up to 40 years |

Number of black rhinos alive

1,000,000

800,000

600,000

400,000

200,000

1,900
0

1900    Now

Year

# World Danger Table

| | Number that may have been alive 100 years ago | Number that may be alive today |
|---|---|---|
| Giant panda | 65,000 | 650 |
| Bengal tiger | 100,000 | 4,500 |
| Blue whale | 335,000 | 4,000 |
| Mountain gorilla | 85,000 | 500 |
| Florida manatee | 75,000 | 2,000 |

There are thousands of other animals in the world that are in danger of becoming **extinct**. This table shows some of these animals.

# How Can You Help the Black Rhino?

If you and your friends raise money for the rhinos, you can send it to these groups. They will take the money and use it to pay guards, and to buy food and tools to help save the black rhino.

Defenders of Wildlife
1101 Fourteenth Street, N.W. #1400
Washington, DC 20005

International Rhino Foundation
14000 International Rd.
Cumberland, OH 43732

World Wildlife Fund
1250 Twenty-fourth Street, N.W.
P.O. Box 97180
Washington, DC 20037

# More Books to Read

Fichter, George S. *Endangered Animals.* New York, N.Y.: Golden Books Publishing Company, 1995.

National Wildlife Federation Staff. *Endangered Species: Wild & Rare.* Broomall, Penn.: Chelsea House Publishers, 1999. An older reader can help you with this book.

# Glossary

| | |
|---|---|
| **dagger** | sharp, pointed knife with a handle |
| **endangered** | group of animals that is dying out, so there are few left |
| **extinct** | group of animals that has completely died out and can never live again |
| **female** | girl or woman |
| **ground** | crushed into powder |
| **herbivore** | animal that eats only plants |
| **herd** | group of the same animals living together |
| **law** | rule or something you have to do |
| **mammal** | warm-blooded animals, like humans, that feed their young on their mother's milk |
| **male** | boy or man |
| **mate** | when a male animal and a female animal come together to make baby animals |
| **poacher/poaching** | hunter who makes money from hunting (poaching) animals to sell parts of their bodies like teeth, bones, and fur |
| **predator** | animal that hunts and kills other animals |
| **protected** | kept safe |
| **savannah** | large area of grassland with few trees |
| **species** | group of living things that are very similar |

# Index